Goblin sharks

CHRISTINE THOMAS ALDERMAN

D1212409

BLACK RABBIT BOOKS

Bolt is published by Black Rabbit Books
P.O. Box 3263, Mankato, Minnesota, 56002.
www.blackrabbitbooks.com
Copyright © 2020 Black Rabbit Books

Marysa Storm, editor; Grant Gould, designer;
Omay Ayres, photo researcher

Library of Congress Cataloging-in-Publication Data
Names: Alderman, Christine Thomas, author.
Title: Goblin sharks / by Christine Thomas Alderman.
Description: Mankato, Minnesota : Black Rabbit Books, [2020] |
Series: Bolt. Swimming with sharks | Audience: Age 8-12. |
Audience: Grade 4 to 6. | Includes bibliographical references and index.
Identifiers: LCCN 2018036399 (print) | LCCN 2018037371 (ebook) |
ISBN 9781680728682 (e-book) | ISBN 9781680728620 (library binding) |
ISBN 9781644660478 (paperback)
Subjects: LCSH: Goblin shark–Juvenile literature.
Classification: LCC QL638.95.M58 (ebook) |
LCC QL638.95.M58 A43 2020 (print) | DDC 597.3/4-dc23
LC record available at https://lccn.loc.gov/2018036399

Printed in the United States. 1/19

Image Credits

Alamy: Paulo Oliveira, 20; Steve Woods
Photography, 18 (sand tiger); china.org.cn:
China.org.cn, 6 (shark); commons.wikimedia.org: An-
drea.dematteis.1987, 14; fishesofaustralia.net.au: Museum
Victoria, 28–29; global.hokudai.ac.jp: Okinawa Churashima
Foundation, 6–7, 29 (shark); imgur.com: rufiooo, 11; noaa.
gov: NOAA, 24; seaparadise.co.jp: Hakkeijima Sea Paradise, 26–27;
seapics.com: David Shen, Cover; Makoto Hirose, 1, 12–13, 18–19,
21, 32; Masa Ushioda, 8–9, 19 (goblin); Shutterstock: Brilliance stock,
17 (fish); Catmando, 19 (tiger); Evlakhov Valeriy, 17 (shrimp); JIANG
HONGYAN, 17 (octopus, squid); Kletr, 19 (hammerhead); Maquiladora,
3 (sharks); Michael Rosskothen, 18 (great white); Rich Carey, 17 (bkgd);
VectorPlotnikoff, 3 (reef bkgd); Vladimir Arndt, 23 (bkgd); WIRACHAI-
PHOTO, 17 (crab); Yongcharoen_kittiyaporn, 6 (bkgd), 14 (bkgd),
29 (bkgd); Zynatis, Cover; sketchfab.com: rstr_tv, 18 (bull); tumblr.
com: veneightor, 17 (goblin); twitter.com: rfedortsov, 22–23;
zatsugaku-news.com: Tomonori Hamada, 4–5
Every effort has been made to contact copyright hold-
ers for material reproduced in this book. Any
omissions will be rectified in subsequent
printings if notice is given to the
publisher.

Contents

 Swimming Along

A strange shark swims slowly along the ocean floor. Its long **snout** slices through the water. Thornlike teeth fill its mouth. This goblin shark looks like a nightmare. And it's on the hunt.

The shark senses a fish. Quickly, its jaw shoots out, grabbing the **prey**. Its neck balloons as the shark swallows the meal. Finished, the fearsome shark snaps its jaw back.

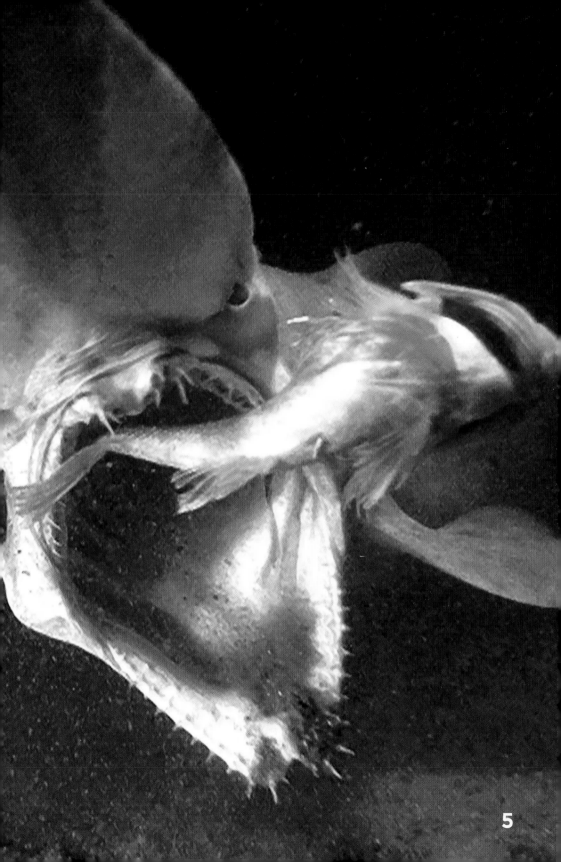

WEIGHT

UP TO 463 POUNDS

(210 kilograms)

Animal or Alien?

Goblin sharks don't look like most sharks. A goblin shark's head is very unusual. Its snout sticks out from its mouth. Like its body, the shark's snout is long and skinny. This shark has a special jaw too. When attacking, the jaw moves forward and its sharp teeth pierce prey.

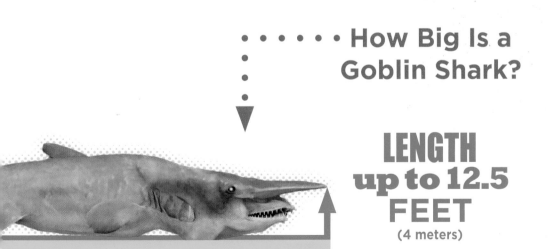

· · · · · · **How Big Is a Goblin Shark?**

LENGTH up to 12.5 FEET
(4 meters)

SMALL EYES

SOFT, FLABBY SKIN

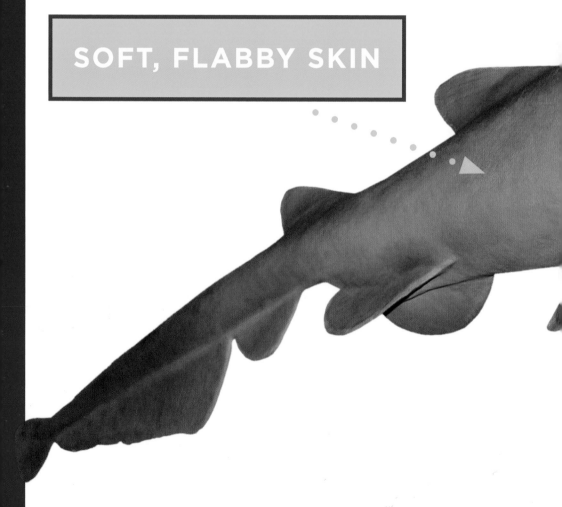

LONG SNOUT

EXTENDABLE JAW

PINKISH-GRAY COLOR

CHAPTER 2

Where They Live
and
What They Eat

Scientists believe goblin sharks live all over the world. They don't know for sure because few have ever been found. These sharks swim deep in the ocean. Most live deeper than divers can go. It's very dark there too. Scientists have a hard time studying them.

People discovered the goblin shark near Japan in 1898. They named the shark after a **mythical** goblin.

WHERE GOBLIN SHARKS HAVE BEEN FOUND

Goblin sharks have been seen or caught in these places.

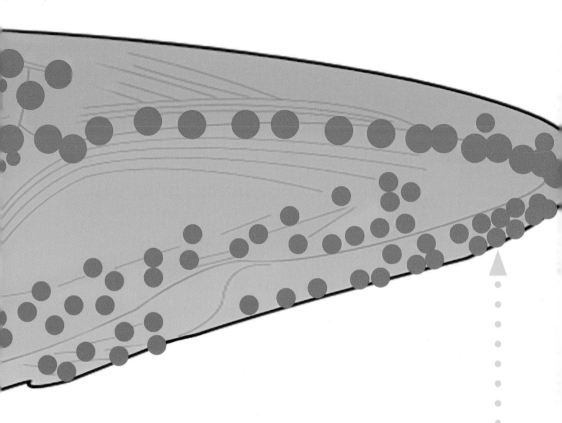

Dining in the Dark

Goblin sharks are made to find food in the dark. They can't rely on sight. So they use **sensors** on their snouts. Goblins use the sensors to find electricity created by prey.

Built for Hunting

Goblins have tools to catch prey too. Their jaws help them attack quickly. And their teeth are perfect for snagging slippery food. These sharks eat fish and **crustaceans**. They also eat octopuses and squid.

What Goblin Sharks Eat

crabs

fish

octopuses

shrimp

squid

SHARKS BY DEPTH

Different types of sharks swim at different depths in the water.

feet below surface	BULL SHARK	SAND TIGER SHARK	GREAT WHITE SHARK
0			
500			
1,000			
1,500	surface to 492 feet (150 m)	shallow water to 625 feet (191 m)	surface to more than 820 feet (250 m)
2,000			
2,500			
3,000			
3,500			
4,000			
4,500			

HAMMERHEAD SHARK

TIGER SHARK

GOBLIN SHARK

surface to about 902 feet [275 m]

shallow water to 1,148 feet [350 m]

131 to 4,265 feet [40 to 1,300 m]

CHAPTER 3

Family Life

Scientists know little about how goblin sharks act. Most sharks live alone, though. Scientists think goblin sharks probably live and hunt alone too. These sharks probably only meet to **mate**.

Prepared Pups

No one has ever seen a **pregnant** goblin shark. But scientists think they give birth to live young. Similar sharks also give birth to live young.

Shark babies are called pups. Pups can hunt right after birth. They don't need their mothers' help. Goblin mothers probably leave their babies after they're born.

Many sharks swim close to shore to give birth.
Goblins might do the same.

CHAPTER 4

Keeping Sharks Safe

Most sharks are at the top of the food chain. Other ocean animals don't hunt them. Their biggest enemy is people. These sharks sometimes get caught in fishing line. They can't swim away and die.

Still Swimming

Scientists do not know how many goblin sharks exist. They know little about them. But they do know people need to care for these sharks' homes.

People must keep the oceans clean. Sharks were on Earth long before humans were. It's up to people to make sure they stick around.

By the Numbers

MORE THAN 500
ESTIMATED NUMBER OF ALL SHARK SPECIES

ABOUT 100 MILLION
NUMBER OF SHARKS KILLED BY HUMANS EACH YEAR (ALL KINDS)

10

TOTAL NUMBER
OF GILLS

3.5 feet
(1 m)

SHORTEST GOBLIN SHARK
EVER FOUND

crustacean (kruh-STEY-shuhn)—a type of animal, such as a crab or lobster, that has several pairs of legs and a body made up of sections covered in a hard outer shell

extendable (ek-STEND-uh-buhl)—able to spread or stretch forth

mate (MAYT)—to join together to produce young

mythical (MITH-i-kuhl)—existing only in the imagination

pregnant (PREG-nuhnt)—carrying one or more unborn offspring in the body

prey (PRAY)—an animal hunted or killed for food

sensor (SEN-sor)—something that finds heat, light, sound, motion, or other things

snout (SNOUT)—the projecting part of an animal's face that includes the nose or nose and mouth

species (SPEE-seez)—a class of individuals that have common characteristics and share a common name

BOOKS

Best, Arthur. *Sharks.* Migrating Animals. New York: Cavendish Square, 2019.

Hull, Joyce A. *Deepwater Sharks.* The Amazing World of Sharks. Broomall, PA: Mason Crest, 2019.

Mason, Paul. *World's Weirdest Sharks.* Wild World of Sharks. Minneapolis: Hungry Tomato, 2018.

WEBSITES

Alien Sharks: Goblin Shark
www.discovery.com/tv-shows/shark-week/videos/alien-sharks-goblin-shark

Goblin Shark
kids.nationalgeographic.com/animals/goblin-shark/#goblin-shark-jaw.jpg

Goblin Shark
www.floridamuseum.ufl.edu/fish/discover/species-profiles/mitsukurina-owstoni

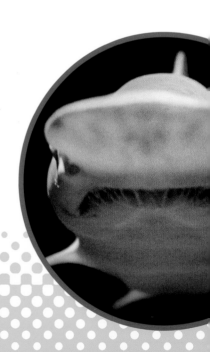